HOW TO PROLONG YOUR JOB SEARCH

HOW TO
PROLONG
YOUR JOB SEARCH

A Humorous Guide to the Pitfalls of Resume Writing

by

PETER S. HERZOG

Abandoned Ladder Press

To Amy, Jenna & Ryan – My Life!

———————————

Also, to Norman G., whose continued support and friendship
has helped make our daily madness into more than just a job.

Table of Contents

Chapter *1*

Introduction

Everyone has opinions about the how's and why's of resume writing. I am certainly no different. Hopefully, my twenty-three years as a "headhunter," as well as the scrutiny of tens of thousands of resumes, lends me credibility.

Throughout my career, I have spent a considerable amount of time imploring executives to see my applicants. This task has not been made easier by the quality of resumes that have come across my desk. Some have made me laugh, some cry, but few have impressed.

On numerous occasions I have either had to suggest changes on applicants' resumes or help tailor them appropriately for a specific position. As their advocate, it is part of my job. That is certainly more effective than explaining to a possible suitor that "the applicant really is a lot better than the resume presented." But most people, rightfully, do not use recruiters as their sole means of job hunting. They should be used as a supplement to their own search and networking. Either way, wouldn't you want the odds in your favor? Well, this obviously starts with the resume.

I will keep it simple. Design your "personal profile" with the mindset that the people reading it are doing so at five minutes to 5 o'clock on a Friday, right before their vacation. The point is to make it easy for them to get to the crux of your experience and background so that they will want to revisit it.

Hiring managers, when they are looking to narrow down their pile of resumes or e-mails, are looking for a fast way out. This means they will find myriad reasons to put yours on the back burner or the "to be considered later" pile. Also, other than human resources recruiters, the hiring

1

process is only a tiny percentage of the decision makers' everyday duties (and probably not their favorite).

It has become apparent to me after many years, that most employment seekers approach resume writing from the wrong angle. Many use artistic license to have their "work of art" stand out from the pack. The resume, however, is not an appropriate forum for this mode of expression. The purpose of it is to get an introduction for a job. It is not a substitute for the interview itself.

The misconception is that including some cute gimmick or fancy sentence will give you an advantage. **NO WAY!** The person reading it, most likely, does not know who you are. Plus, you cannot possibly know their nuances, current mood or preferences. So, keep everything basic, straightforward and uncomplicated.

I understand that resume preparation is a very subjective process. Some like input from every source. Others do not want any help at all. After you have agonized to create what you deem an appropriate profile of your accomplishments, you do not want family, friends, business associates, educators and/or recruiters ripping it apart. That is where I am hoping to be of help.

This is not another resume writing book updating or introducing the latest trend. My theory is different. While I will supply you with certain parameters, the focus is primarily on what <u>NOT</u> to do. I believe once you can identify the potential hazards, the "how to" part is common sense. This isn't brain surgery.

There are always exceptions to the rule, but the rudimentary breakdown of the resume, to be discussed, covers what I believe are the majority of scenarios. The sample excerpts to be presented, while somewhat extreme, are not made up (identifying characteristics were changed or removed to protect the innocent). Many of them are humorous but were included to impress on the reader what to avoid.

The contents of your resume will not be enhanced just because the style being used is unique or has flair. Keep your eye on the ball as the goal is to obtain an interview. The focus should always remain on your background. Do not detract from that (unless you are *trying* to create a diversion).

Chapter 2

Cover Letter

The cover letter is your opening statement and should be concise and to the point. To be quite honest, they are rarely paid much attention to. This is especially true if they duplicate what is in your resume. There are some that stand out but not because they are viewed in a positive light.

The following introduction, which was sent to me a few years ago, is one of those examples. It is my all-time favorite. To this day, I still pull it out any time I need a chuckle.

Example:

Dear Mr. Herzog:

I have put my MS Word to work to let you know that I am alive, well and lusting for a better opportunity....

If you can assist me to find a sterling position in New York or in any number of cities and states that include Philadelphia, Houston, Dallas, San Francisco, Seattle, Los Angeles, Denver, Montreal, Boston, Chicago, D.C. and California, Texas, Illinois, Florida, Oregon, Washington, Hawaii, Massachusetts and Arizona among others– if you may do this I will be a very happy camper....

I am "great" at finding jobs for others. But, I need assistance when it comes to me. The last go-around took 3,000 contacts to get one offer in New York, one in Virginia, one in Thailand and one in South America..... But, when I had a billion dollar portfolio management offer in hand at a Midwestern bank, the offer fell apart at one minute to midnight since there was a feeling I might not be sufficiently challenged.

I should have done better. One of your clients or associates may find my pristine background of interest–and help me do better!

Very truly yours,

...

My Opinion:

◇ Could I make this up? My jaw still scrapes the ground when I read it. By the way, I think he left out Nebraska!

The previous letter actually gave me the impetus to write this book. After reading it, I became convinced that if there is one message that I can pass on to job seekers it would be: **DON'T BE CUTE**. This goes for the cover letter, resume and of course, the interview. It is not beneficial. In most cases, you get one chance. If you attempt to be funny or sarcastic with your initial presentation, the door will be shut before it was even ajar. Keep it basic and know what you want to say.

The longer the cover letter or introductory e-mail, the more likely it will be deleted or sent to the recycle bin (previously known as the circular file prior to the universally accepted e-mail/online application process). Ideally, it should not be more than three paragraphs and can include (if applicable):

1. Why you are sending the resume

2. How (or from whom) you heard about the opening

3. Something specific that cannot be inferred from your resume (*i.e.* work situation, special skill, kind of job you are looking for, etc.)

4. Current compensation (base, bonus and any other forms of remu-neration, *i.e.* stock, options, etc.) if you are responding to an ad or posting, recruiter or human resources executive. Avoid stating what kind of compensation you are looking for (unless mandated). There are many components to a salary package and it may not be obvious to the person who is reading/screening your cover letter what you are referring to. It could rule you out.

Be brief!

Example:

Dear Recruiter:

I would like to take this opportunity to introduce myself to you. My name is Maria D. and here is another resume for your collection. Are you looking for a *delinquent*, consistently dedicated employee? Then look no further, I'm your person......

My Opinion:

◇ I believe this type of introduction is a turn-off but more importantly, the biggest *faux pas* one can make is not proofreading. Spelling mistakes (easily corrected by spell check), word omissions and incorrect usage are not tolerable and could mean immediate disqualification. In this example, I am pretty certain that she did not mean to say "delinquent." OUCH! Obviously, she wanted to convey the word "diligent." Although it made me laugh, her resume was never to be seen again.

Example:

The following is an introduction from an applicant with a total of four years of limited experience (two years in operations/trade support for a major investment bank and two years doing a variety of temporary assignments):

Dear Mr. Herzog:

At present, having considered my personal goals, I am beginning the job hunt. Your agency, which was referred to me by a friend, is on my short list.

I have discussed my decision to look for a new job with both my manager and my H.R. representative. Each of them has helped me investigate opportunities within Merrill Lynch, and I understand why the "Firm" wants me to stay: no matter how loose the labor market, there is always a scarcity of talented and motivated personnel. You will see from my resume that I have shown a history of hustle, promotability, and drive to achieve in a variety of fields.

Having invested more than two years with Merrill Lynch, I am ready to move on and up within the industry. Once you have reviewed my resume, you will surely want to learn more about me. Your efforts certainly are appreciated and will be rewarded amply.

My Opinion:

◇ I "surely" did not want to learn more about him. His background is not that impressive to warrant being arrogant and cocky. Actually, this type of cover letter is never appropriate, no matter what the level of the candidate. He had a strike against him before I even glanced at his resume. Next time, try being a bit more humble.

Example: (last two paragraphs of a two page cover letter–I just could not resist)

.......I do not believe that I could have averted the 2008 financial meltdown or the collapse of Lehman Brothers. However, I am confident that I can certainly help my employer make a lot of money.

Please be advised that over 115 inches of snow and extremely cold temperatures in the Boston area during the past winter gave me a bad taste for winter in the Northeast. For this reason, my geographical preference will be the South or Southwest, specifically the states of Florida or Arizona. However, a challenging job opportunity in Alaska would not deter my spirits.

My Opinion:

◇ What a snow job! I hope that my delete button is not stuck.

Chapter 3

Address

Example:

I. M. Crazy

(212) 555-0406

Gotta-Get-A-Job, USA

222 No Way

PROFESSIONAL OBJECTIVE:

Secure a position at a financial institution to further develop my skills in the area of banking and finance

WORK EXPERIENCE:

BANKERS REGISTRY   **August 2005 – Present**
➤ Long term assignment at Astoria Federal Savings Bank as loan processing agent – Prepared and generated applications, appraisals and credit reports; daily interaction with clients

PFI FINANCIAL SERVICES   **August 2003 – January 2005**
Loan Processor/Mortgage Consultant
➤ Reviewed financial statements and analyzed credit reports to determine potential client merit
➤ Supervised work flow for two satellite offices
➤ Prepared & packaged loan applications for bank processing
➤ Entered data for computer generated financial reports
➤ Organized sales trips for mortgage auctions

J. FINCH & COMPANY   **August 2002 – July 2003**
Assistant Broker
➤ Pre-qualified potential investors to meet set criteria
➤ Prepared financial statements in Word

QUEENS COLLEGE   **October 1998 – May 2000**
Office Assistant
➤ Prepared computer reports involving purchase orders and work requests
➤ Office filing, handled phone requests and various projects as assigned

EDUCATION:

Queens College, 2002 – BBA, Finance

SPECIAL SKILLS:

Microsoft Office Suite, Ability to analyze financial materials; Excellent communication and interpersonal skills

REFERENCES: Available Upon Request

My Opinion:

◇ Are you kidding? Is this person a megalomaniac? Does putting your name in monster letters serve any purpose? What it does accomplish is taking the focus away from everything else on the resume as well as raising questions about the applicant.

In an ideal world, there should not have to be a chapter on one's name and address. But as seen from this example, always expect the unexpected.

There is only one place for your name and address and that is ON TOP. If desired, 1) put your name in bold face and/or regular caps and 2) include your full address plus home, work (optional), and/or cell phone numbers as well as e-mail address, but do not highlight (bold) these.

That is it. Simple! As a matter of fact, so simple that I will not insult your intelligence by giving you a good example. You are on your own with this one.

Chapter 4

Objective: Leave Out

This section contains my biggest pet peeve when it comes to resume writing. I have yet to see an Objective, or for that matter, sections titled Summary, Profile or Qualifications, that helps promote a candidate. For example, why would an accountant have an Objective that says, "To obtain a growth-oriented position in accounting"? Does this mean as opposed to a stagnant one? It just sounds ridiculous.

Some helpful suggestions:

1. If there is some extenuating circumstance or point of information that you must get across, then say it in a cover letter.

2. When you send a resume for a particular position, let's assume that you are somewhat qualified for it. So, there is no need to be redundant and state the obvious in an Objective.

3. It will look foolish if you are applying for a spot that is even slightly different than your Objective.

4. Everyone wants a "successful career," "challenging position," "advancement" or "professional growth." Also, we hope that everyone is "dedicated and hard working," "diligent," "gets along with others" and wants "to utilize their acquired knowledge." Including these statements will not have any impact. You will not be hired just from a resume. Remember, there is a *little* process known as interviewing where you will be required to get your attributes across.

5. The only time I would even remotely recommend using a Summary or Profile section would be with a *functional resume*. This is a type of resume that gives an overview of one's background followed by a list of their jobs (without descriptions) and dates of employment. This is rarely used and only, possibly, if someone has had many jobs, especially in a relatively short period of time.

Example:

OBJECTIVE: To get a good job

My Opinion:

◇ Not bad for one of life's overall aspirations, but what would you think if you saw this on the first line of a resume !?!

Example:

OBJECTIVE: Seeking a challenging opportunity that best utilizes my experience and strengths for the benefit of the company

My Opinion:

◇ How altruistic of this candidate. PHONY!

Example:

PROFILE: Frequently extolled for perseverance, leadership, maturity and ability to comprehend information quickly. Persuasive, multi-lingual speaker with self-confidence and solid communicative ability. Excellent written and interpersonal skills. Often praised for being bright, motivated, aggressive and responsible.

My Opinion:

◇ Can this person also walk on water? A little overpowering and egotistical, don't you think? If this person is lucky, his Profile will be ignored and his experience as presented on the resume, will land him an interview. Otherwise, count on the resume being discarded.

Example:

OBJECTIVE:
To obtain a stimulating position in the field of finance

My Opinion:

◇ Is it just me that gets annoyed at reading this? I cannot wait for the day that someone's Objective says the following:

OBJECTIVE:
To obtain a job where I can do the same thing every day and get home as quickly as possible

Now that would stand out!

Chapter 5

Education

Example:

University of Wisconsin
Madison, Wisconsin

M.S. - Finance and Banking, May 2010
Concentration: Quantitative Modeling

Ph.D. - Computer Sciences, May 2008
Concentration: Operations Research / Mathematical Programming

M.S. - Computer Sciences, May 2006
Concentration: Operating Systems and Data Structures

Beijing University
Beijing, China

M.S. - Mathematical Sciences, August 2001
Concentration: Stochastic Processes and Statistics

B.S. - Mathematical Sciences, August 1998

My Opinion:

◇ Five degrees, not too bad. A veritable rocket scientist. That is an impressive beginning to a resume, don't you agree?

This is an example, albeit extreme, as to why one would list Education prior to Experience. Another would be if you have recently (within one year) completed a degree and have little or no work experience (usually, no more than two years). Once you have more than two years of relevant work experience, and sooner in some cases, its significance is multiplied and should be reflected by positioning it above Education. In this situation, "relevant" is defined as consistent with your education or with the job for which you are applying.

Example:

EDUCATION
> **Rutgers University**, Newark, N.J.
> B.S. Finance, June 2010
> GPA: 3.5/4.0 *Cum Laude*

HONORS
> National Business Honor Society
> Dean's List - 5 Semesters

EXPERIENCE
> **Midlantic Bank, N.A.**, Edison, NJ
> *Corporate Credit Analyst*
> September 2010 to Present
> – Formally credit trained in the Commercial
>   Analysis for Lenders Program
> – Analyze financial statements to determine
>   credit worthiness of corporate banking clients
> – Accompany senior loan officers on calls
> – Make loan presentations to senior management

INTERNSHIPS
> **Smith Barney Shearson**, Newark, N.J.
> Sales Assistant
> November 2009 to February 2010

My Opinion:

◇ This is a good format for a recent college graduate with minimal experience.

◇ After the mid-to-end of 2012 it would become appropriate to switch Education and Experience.

Example:

EDUCATION

COLUMBIA BUSINESS SCHOOL
MBA - Finance and Capital, May 2011
Investment Club and Sales and Trading Club

EMORY UNIVERSITY
BA - Economics, May 2007
Fund Raiser, Emory Alumni Association

EXPERIENCE

2008 - 2010   **Chase Investment Services**, New York, NY
Management Trainee

     * Rotations within marketing, compliance,
       operations and sales
     * Completed training to be sales support's
       fixed income specialist
     * Tracked fixed income securities and
       mutual fund positions

2007   **Bankers Trust Company**, New York, NY
Global Funding - Product Specialist

My Opinion:

◇ This is a good format for a recent, full-time, Masters graduate.

◇ The omission of months under Experience is misleading as to the actual length of time, but we will assume (at most) 2-3 years.

◇ The same format can be used in the uncommon scenario of 4+ years of experience prior to completing a full-time graduate program.

◇ In cases where there might be part-time education, positioning should be in the Education section below Experience (this includes upon completion of the degree).

Example:

EDUCATION
1995   **UNIVERSITY OF MIAMI**,
                    GRADUATE SCHOOL OF BUSINESS
                    ADMINISTRATION, Florida
                    MBA, Marketing

                    PENN STATE UNIVERSITY, Pennsylvania
                    BA, Magna Cum Laude, History
                    Pennsylvania Alumnae Club
                    Award for Most Creative Women Graduate in 1990.

CAREER HISTORY
2007-Present   **GOLDMAN SACHS & CO.**, New York
                    <u>Management Trainee</u>: Responsible for
                    pre-publication approval of all research; bond
                    portfolio analysis, convertibles, equity, equity
                    portfolio analysis, derivatives, fixed income,
                    emerging markets, politics: manifolds,
                    reports and financing summaries.

2003-2007   **MORGAN CORPORATION**, New Jersey
                    <u>Marketing Consulting</u>: Responsible for developing
                    a marketing plan including: market analysis and
                    strategic planning, redesign of corporate identity;
                    writing and designing technical literature and
                    product catalog.

1997-2001   **STEIN & STEIN**, Virginia
                    CERTIFIED PUBLIC ACCOUNTANTS,
                    <u>Junior Accountant</u>

My Opinion:

◇ There are numerous errors in this partial resume (including formatting issues to be discussed later) but I used it to highlight the incorrect positioning of Education and Career History. Think it through. There is no possible reason to present it in this manner. At this stage

16

of one's career it should be crystal clear that the hiring emphasis will be on your experience in the work place.

Do not get the impression that I am downplaying the overall importance of education. From secretarial school to Ph.D. programs, it is the foundation of everyone's career. Also, top or "Ivy League" institutions obviously carry a lot of weight. But in today's stagnant economy, experience - and especially very specific experience - must be stressed. One reason for this is that companies are cutting costs to hire and train personnel, so new hires must be able to hit the ground running. Make it easier for the decision makers. Let your work history jump out at them.

Example:

EDUCATION

09/92 - 06/95	B.S. in Mathematics, National Cheng Kung University
06/97 - 12/99	M.S. in Mathematics, Xavier University
12/99 - 08/04	Ph.D. in Statistics, Xavier University
01/09 - 12/10	M.B.A., University of Cincinnati

My Opinion:

◇ In this scenario, is the B.S. degree the most significant? I certainly hope not. As we all know, common sense is not always in direct proportion to the amount of one's education. Always list more than one degree in descending order (most recent first).

Example:

EDUCATION   Business Administration

My Opinion:

◇ I know that I have preached simplicity and to be concise, but this is ridiculous! Feel free to add a little more information.

Example:

EDUCATION

University of Maryland, College Park, MD
B.A. – Communications (I think), June 2005

My Opinion: (sad, but true)

◇ I think!?! I think not!

Chapter 6

Experience

Example:

12/08 - Present	<u>Homemaker</u> and <u>Childcare</u> <u>Provider</u>

Responsible for day-to-day childcare and household management including: budgeting and purchasing of goods and supplies, preparing daily and weekly recreational and educational activities, monitoring and assisting with home work assignments and preparing nutritional meals.

6/05 - 11/08	<u>Marine</u> <u>Midland</u> <u>Bank</u>, New York, NY Receptionist / Secretary

My Opinion:

◇ My first impression was that she was running a day care business for a number of children. After further analysis, it turned out to be a resourceful way of explaining a potential gap on her resume for the time period when she raised her own child. This was a pleasant surprise and smart idea. If the "Homemaker" description was not included, a "red flag" would have been raised and a potential employer would question the gap since her last position. Having it clears up any confusion and could very well keep her in the running to be called for an interview.

Experience, Experience, Experience. As I have alluded to in prior chapters, this is where your focus always should be in any economic environment, whether a strong or weak one. Even if you have light or only internship experience, the description and format can make a difference. As seen from the previous example, there is a description that is appropriate for everything that we have done. It does not matter if you are an administrative assistant or Managing Director. The key is to know when to include certain descriptions or exclude them, and when to expand or cut them down. In most cases it should be obvious.

Example:

EXPERIENCE

NATIONAL WESTMINSTER BANK, N.A.
2002 - Present

Vice President, Credit Risk Evaluation

* Analyze, review and make recommendations on corporate finance applications focusing on leverage finance, asset-securitization and project finance

My Opinion:

◇ That was the entire description for his most current position. Not a bad opening sentence but he is a Vice President and probably has more functions. Be creative and extrapolate! He doesn't do himself justice by making the presentation in this manner. Even if prior positions were similar, spend more time on recent duties and accomplishments (*i.e.* managerial duties, special projects, notable sales/transactions, etc.). At the V.P. level, you have attained a certain status and have the "green light" to talk more about yourself.

Example:

EXPERIENCE

May 2004-Present   **K Mart, Inc.**, South Plainfield, N.J.
                                  Customer Service - Assistant Manager

* Handle customer inquiries and resolve complaints
* Orientation of new employees and allocation of job responsibilities
* Liaison between employees and store manager to negotiate personal issues
* Assist with inventory and price controls of merchandise
* Enter, update and maintain product history and pricing on internal computer system

My Opinion:

◇ What a wonderful description! It is obvious that this person took the time and a modicum of effort to portray her job responsibilities in a cogent manner. She came across as very professional. It is much more impressive than the prior Vice President example.

Here is some friendly advice about the body of the resume:

A) Make sure to use the bullet format. This means using a *, −, or • before each sentence under each position listed. Paragraph form can be cumbersome and awkward to read. This is partially due to poor grammar, incorrect punctuation and run-on sentences that are common mistakes when experience is presented this way. So, break down any paragraph that you have written into individual sentences, preceded by a bullet. Remember, we want to make it easy to read.

Note: If a name of a company that you are listing is unrecognizable, then including a brief description of the company before your title and job function is appropriate, as the following demonstrates:

The Norinchukin Bank, Ltd., New York, NY
Japanese Commercial Bank - 81st largest bank (ranked by assets) in the world
Assistant Vice President - Real Estate Finance Group

*......................job function........................

B) One page resumes, well-spaced and aesthetically pleasing, are always preferred. However, the longer one is in the work force, more experience is usually attained and one page might not be feasible. In these cases (8+ years is a good benchmark, but it will vary) two pages can be used. Try not to use two full pages (or more). Nobody wants to read a book on your life.

Example:

EDUCATION   St. Michael's College, Colchester, Vermont
B.A. in Psychology *magna cum laude*; May 2011
Secondary concentrations in Spanish and statistics
G.P.A. 3.60, G.P.A. in major 3.80   Dean's List
• Costa Rican studies Program, San Jose, Costa Rica.   May 2010.
• Youth in Britain Program, London.   January 2010.
• SUNY Albany, Albany, New York.   2007-2008.

HONORS/   Psi Chi, National Psychology Honor Society (Charter member)
LEADERSHIP   Who's Who Among American College Students (2011)
Vice President Snowboard Club, SUNY Albany
Founder/President Meditation Club, SUNY Albany

President, The Psychological Society, St. Michael's College. Planned and
coordinated meetings and activities of a 50+ member student organization
promoting awareness of career opportunities, graduate school,
psychological and social issues. 2010-2011.

WORK   Intern, MBIA, Municipal Investors Service Corporation, Armonk, N.Y.
EXPERIENCE   Assisted Sr. Director of Marketing and maintained client profiles in a
Windows based computer system. Assisted client service desk in investment
relations and answered phones. Fall 2010.

Research Assistant, Human Behavioral Pharmacology Laboratory. University
of Vermont, Burlington, Vt. Prepared and administered test materials,
recorded and analyzed data, and recruited participants. Incorporated
research design and data analysis techniques in original research
proposal. Jan. – July 2010.

Student Assistant/Cultural Facilitator, Center for International Programs,
St. Michael's College. Served as a translator, mentor, and guide for
Colombian high school students studying the English language and American
culture. Oct. 2009 and May 2010.

Office Assistant, Great Neck Women's Medical Care, Great Neck, N.Y.
Confirmed appointments, answered phones, and filed patients charts.
Processed data on computer. Summer 2009.

VOLUNTEER   Women Helping Battered Women, Burlington, Vt. Gathered relevant data of
EXPERIENCE   350 women, analyzed and graphed information with NCSS and Quattro Pro,
then wrote an original research paper to determine effectiveness of
agency. Fall 2010 - Spring 2011.

Best Buddies, St. Michael's College. Volunteer companion to a
developmentally disabled young woman. Spring 2011.

North Shore Creative Rehabilitation Center Inc., Great Neck, N.Y.
Participated in staff and community meetings and group therapy sessions.,
Facilitated group sessions and assisted clients in life skills training
and group outings. Summer 2009.

SKILLS   Microsoft Word. Ami Pro 3.0, Microsoft Works
Excel, Quattro Pro 4.0, NCSS. Internet
Strong working knowledge of Spanish

INTERESTS   Snowboarding, figure skating, running, and tennis.

REFERENCES   Available upon request.

My Opinion:

◇ Did you get dizzy, as I did, from trying to read that? Also, did you realize that this is a resume of a recent college graduate? What do you think it will look like when she has a few years of full-time work experience?

This is an excellent example how detailed descriptions of everything that you have done (especially over a short period of time) do not need to be included. Either cut out half of the resume or be brief with each situation. If your resume cannot be read without two aspirin, then it won't matter what you have accomplished.

Here are some more helpful hints along the same theme of avoiding overcrowded resumes:

1. If you have 15+ years of work experience then your first job does not need to be included, especially if it was only 1-2 years and if it was unrelated to your current industry.

2. If you have 3+ years of work experience, summer jobs (*i.e.* camp counselor or lifeguard) do not need to be included. On the other hand, internships that are related to your current industry can still be added.

3. A full-time job that lasted 3 months or less (unless it was your only position) does not need to be included.

Note: These omissions will not hurt your chances of getting an introduction. If asked about, they can be discussed in an application or interview.

C) Chronological resumes, which list positions with their descriptions in descending (present first) order, are highly preferred. Functional resumes, as previously stated, are only appropriate if intended to take the focus away from a jumpy background.

D) If applying for a job within the same industry, include numbers in the description that are easily understood and impressive, if appropriate. For example:

- Manage a portfolio of $750MM
- Billed over $500k in 2010

- Company's largest producer the past four years
- Market to Fortune 1000 companies with a minimum of $1B in sales

E) One of the most common and annoying errors is the incorrect usage of word tense. Avoid this by paying attention to detail and being consistent. Obviously, *use the present tense when describing current positions and the past tense with previous spots.*

F) Many professionals design more than one resume, gearing each towards a specific opening. Subtle changes and emphasizing a certain expertise can make the difference. This is definitely more appropriate than being general or vague in your description and addressing your job preference in an Objective.

G) Here are some commonly used "buzz" words that might help you get started:

analyze(d)	apply(ied)	assess(ed)	assist(ed)
communicate(d)	conduct(ed)	design(ed)	detail(ed)
develop(ed)	edit(ed)	establish(ed)	evaluate(d)
execute(d)	handle(d)	identify(ied)	interact(ed)
liaison(liaised)	manage(d)	market(ed)	monitor(ed)
negotiate(d)	perform(ed)	provide(d)	responsible for
review(ed)	supervise(d)	support(ed)	utilize(d)

One last example that I just could not leave out:

Employment   10/07 - Present
Senior Programmer Analyst - Major Investment Bank
* Equity trading systems development

My Opinion:

◇ Why would you send a resume without the name of the institution that currently employs you? Is your position classified? Do you work for the CIA? If you are that paranoid with the resume, do not expect many responses.

That was my initial reaction when reading the faxed version of his resume (faxing resumes are not common practice anymore and if sent in this manner now, will certainly get lost). The kicker was when I noticed the fax stamp on top of the resume. Next to date, time and the sending fax number, was the name of his company! How smart was that!?! **GENIUS!**

Note: Six months later he e-mailed me his resume, without realizing that he had sent it to me before - AND, he did it again. It was sent from his work account, with the name of his company in plain sight in the e-mail address! Oh well, at least I get to laugh each day.

Chapter 7

Personal / Accomplishments / Special Skills (and other fluff)

Example:

> **PERSONAL:** Constantly replenished jar of Oreo cookies kept on desk at all times

My Opinion:

◊ Does this mean that after she eats one, a new one is put back in? Would you believe that this was from a resume of a Senior Vice President, right after a long list of honors and awards? I was dumbfounded and aghast. What went into her thought process that concluded this statement was necessary? Ironically, the resume was pretty good up until this last revelation. NOT APPROPRIATE!

As noted from the title of this chapter, there are a variety of sections that are acceptable as supplements to the body of the resume. Unfortunately, this is where an abundance of job seekers take on "poetic license." It seems like anything and everything goes. The caveat: do not taint your entire resume with what might be perceived as a quirk.

At this point of the guideline, I would hope that the general theme is starting to hit home. Keep it simple and use common sense. If it is relevant and/or significant then include it. I hesitate to also use the word "unique" because it is a commonly misused term in this scenario. Unique does not mean (under the Personal or Interest section): "Reading, writing and cycling" or "Full jars of Oreo cookies." The banal and ridiculous can be left out. It could rub the reader the wrong way and diminish your chances of getting an interview. Why take the chance?

Ideas on what to include are (but not limited to):

1. Computer Skills

2. Honors and Awards

3. Associations / Affiliations

4. Licenses (professional, of course, not driver's)

5. Outstanding Achievements, such as:

    a) professional athletics

    b) Olympics participation

    c) Arctic exploration [...I think you get the point]

Example:

Birthdate:	March 21, 1969
Birthplace:	Brussels, Belgium
Height & Weight:	6'2", 205lbs.
Citizen:	French, U.S. Resident
Wife:	Kyoko (Japanese)
Children:	Arthur & Beatrice

My Opinion:

◇ He left out his kids' birthdates. How will I know when to send them their gifts? My father showed me a resume preparation book from over 30 years ago that showed this type of example as the norm. Nowadays it is unacceptable and should be left out.

The **only** exception is for residency status. While most jobs in the U.S. require at least a green card, there are many that will provide job sponsorship depending on one's visa. So, if there is any question as to your residency status, include it. It will take out the guesswork. The other personal tidbits (*i.e.* age, weight and marital status) will not or cannot be asked of you during the interview process.

Example:

Personal * Interests include Constructions with Iron

My Opinion:

◇ Huh?

Examples:

A) **Interests**
Golf (handicap 17) and my family (of course!)

B) **INTERESTS** Golf, Basketball and Antique shopping.
Greatest Asset: My wife

My Opinion:

◇ Oh, please. How corny!

Example:

SPECIAL SKILLS: Highly effective communicator. Likeable, with a manner that instills personal ties and loyalty

My Opinion:

◇ LIKEABLE! Let me be the judge of that, if and when I interview you. A turn-off.

Example:

LICENSES: NASD Series 6 (*expired*), Massachusetts Blue Sky Series 63 (*expired*), Variable Annuity, Life, Health and Property (*expired*)

My Opinion:

◇ Webster's New World Dictionary (Second College Edition) defines "expired" as: "to come to an end; terminate; cease." In other words, no longer of value! There are some who contend that including expired licenses shows the capacity to pass these exams. That might be the case but, guess what? You will have to show that capacity once again. **LOOKS FOOLISH!**

Example:

PERSONAL INTERESTS
Sports: baseball, cycling, tennis, hiking, bowling and Nautilus weight training. Enjoy visiting museums and attending classical concerts. **Comedy fanatic!**

My Opinion:

◇ Regardless of context, would you want to interview someone who is a self-described 'fanatic'? It gives me a queasy feeling.

Example:

Travel Log: Traveled to various cities and learned how to adjust to different locations including: Manila, Philippines; Honolulu, Hawaii; San Francisco, San Diego and Los Angeles, California; Las Vegas and Reno, Nevada; Buffalo and New York, New York

My Opinion:

◇ Adjusting to Hawaii must have been difficult!?! Hire him!

Example:

ADDITIONAL INFORMATION: Experienced in driving during rush hour in the Philippines (especially Manila)

My Opinion:

◇ How about NYC? This is an absolute classic.

Example:

Self-Evaluation Skill Sets:

- computer skills:	highest
- technical skills:	very high
- analytical skills:	very high
- synthesizing skills:	very high
- team work:	quite high
- leadership:	high
- initiative:	extremely high
- creativity:	highest
- time management:	very high
- stress management:	very high
- networking:	high
- people skills:	quite high
- general communication skills:	extraordinary
- public speaking:	extremely high
- business/technical writing:	extraordinary
- international perspective:	broad

- Vision: Do not miss the joy of being, in the
         quest for improvement or being the best!

My Opinion:

◇ Hmmm. I am too exhausted to even try and comment. That should say it all.

Chapter 8

References: Furnished Upon Request

The easiest part of preparing the resume is including the References line. With regard to simplicity, it is in the same category as one's address - or at least it should be. I could go on for a page or more and make up good reasons as to why this is an important finishing touch. Quite honestly, it would be meaningless. I have no idea why it is common practice to have References as an ending, except for it being used as filler. If a prospective employer asks you for references, would you really say no?

Believe it or not, I will not buck the trend on this trite, closing statement. As a matter of fact I usually like seeing it added. The rule of thumb is to include it only if you have the room. Never put the References line in if it means extending your resume to a second page or overcrowding the first. If it is left out, it is not a big deal. I have never heard a positive or negative comment about the inclusion or omission of this line. It is like the human appendix, a vestigial organ. Basically, it is useless.

Alternate

References available upon request

My Opinion:

◇ If you decide to put it in, the "furnished upon request" and the "available upon request" phrases are the only ones that should be used. Do not make it complicated. There's no need to reinvent the wheel.

Examples:

References: Will be furnished for your comfort

References: Eventually will be furnished

References: Will be made available upon command

My Opinion:

◇ Yes, I have seen these examples. What a way to ruin a perfectly good resume. Total nonsense! Remember, being cute on a resume (no matter what section) does not put you in a positive light. It is only a quicker road to the recycle bin.

Chapter 9

Closing

My frustration level got to be too much after many years of reviewing inappropriate resume styles, formats and descriptions. I could not take it anymore. I had a message that had to be heard.

To be serious, there is not just one way to go about writing a resume. Plus, it is very difficult, if not arrogant, to tell someone what the perfect, personal profile looks like. That being said, I realize my critique of some of the examples was harsh. This is because the competition out there is fierce. Let's level the playing field. Ultimately, what you write is a reflection of who you are.

Since there are a variety of opinions and methods on this topic, I felt a new, simplistic approach was necessary. Also, I tried to sprinkle some humor into it to make my points.

My Formula:

A FEW PARAMETERS TO FOLLOW
— KNOWING THE PITFALLS TO AVOID
= AN APPROPRIATE RESUME

The rest is common sense. So, GO FOR IT! Either: 1) start it, 2) amend it, or 3) update it.

I will end this guideline with what I feel is the perfect resume– MY OWN!

PETER S. HERZOG
310 East 46th Street – #7K
New York, NY 10017
w: (212) 661-8300 c: (917) 555-9760
peter@hbcgroupinc.com

EXPERIENCE

The HBC Group, Inc., New York, NY   October 1988 - Present
Executive Placement
Senior Vice President – Corporate Banking Division

- Recruit mid-level to senior-level professionals for top-tier commercial and investment banking positions
- Identify and evaluate candidates and market them to senior management
- Develop new client opportunities while maintaining existing base
- Act as a liaison between line managers and human resources staff
- Provide career counseling
- Prepare candidates extensively for interviews
- Review resumes and tailor them for specific jobs
- Train and manage a recruiting staff of three
- Maintain resume database as well as our website's open job listings
- Key producer of company's record earnings for 14 of the past 15 years
- Developed recruitment sub-specialty within energy risk management

B. Jadow & Sons, Inc., New York, NY   October 1987 – October 1988
Distributor of precision tools and equipment to the jewelry and optical trades
Purchasing Agent

- Co-head of domestic and foreign purchasing for 5,000-item product line
- Negotiated product prices and established wholesale prices
- Established new product lines and vendor accounts

Albany Medical Center Hospital, Albany, NY   June 1986 – June 1987
Supervisor – Radiology Library

- Supervised, trained and scheduled a ten-employee shift
- Extensive database work with patient records
- Interacted daily with departmental heads, doctors and other health-related professionals

EDUCATION

State University of New York at Albany, Albany, NY   May 1986
Bachelor of Arts – Major: Sociology, Minor: Business Administration

COMPUTER SKILLS

Access, SQL (and other customized databases), Excel, PowerPoint, Word and Bloomberg

About the Author

Peter Herzog works in New York City and has been an executive recruiter with the same firm since 1988. He specializes in the placement of banking and finance professionals. As of last count he has reviewed 71,786 resumes. He plans to retire when that number reaches 100,000, unless he loses his mind first.

This is Peter's first publication. He is contemplating writing a book about the interviewing process, but claims the stories he has would read too much like fiction (and nobody would believe him).